To: _____

From _____

The Sky's the Limit, Graduate!

CHRIS SHEA

THOMAS NELSON
Since 1798

NASHVILLE DALLAS MEXICO CITY RIO DE JANEIRO BEIJING

Published in Nashville, Tennessee, by Thomas Nelson. Thomas Nelson is a registered trademark of Thomas Nelson, Inc.

Design by The DesignWorks Group and Robin Black, Blackbird Creative.

Thomas Nelson, Inc., titles may be purchased in bulk for educational, business, fund-raising, or sales promotional use. For information, please e-mail SpecialMarkets@ThomasNelson.com.

ISBN: 978-1-4041-8792-4

www.thomasnelson.com

Printed and bound in China

for Emily Fleming
who'll be one
of the
very best . . .

A   B   C

1   2   3

Isn't it amazing
how far they've
taken you,

1, 2, 3 and ABC?

Numbers turning into
math,

letters turning
into words.

They've carried
you

14

You On Your First Day!!

since your very
first day of school

to where you
stand today
at the threshold
of the
future...

your graduation day!

On waves of algebra
and
spelling,

of reading and biology,

across a sea
of music,

of art,
and history

you've sailed across
your years in school

grade 1

Kindergarden

middle school

high school

college

gathering on your journey
new skills as you needed
them;

learning
long division,

foreign languages
too,

how to write
a term paper

"only god can make a tree."

or memorize

a poem.

You mastered things
    not   taught
         in
      books

like how to throw
a baseball

or work together
with your friends

on a science
presentation.

Everything
you know
today

began with A
B
C

and   when listing

your accomplishments

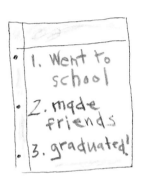

1. Went to school
2. made friends
3. graduated!

you begin with 1
                2
                 3

On your graduation day

I hope you'll capture
vividly

the feelings that
surround you.

I hope you'll see
in retrospect that
the days you
spent in the
company of friends

flew quite
quickly by;

and the teachers
who really taught you
best

were the ones
who expected
the
most.

(and that forever
in your family's heart

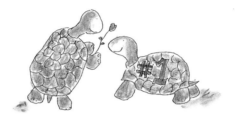

you'll always be
their number one :)

Do you know what
I wish you
most

II

..and the crowd
burst out in
applause.
✦

III

On The
Threshold

The sky shone
blue as topaz
and opportunity
lay ahead like

as one chapter ends

and a brand new one
begins?

I wish you to remember
several simple
things,

46

the ABCs of living,
the 1, 2, 3
of
Life.

A. Never settle.

B. Never lie

(To others or yourself.)

C. And never be...

afraid to try
again.

1. Always count
your blessings

1. Health
2. Friends
3. family
4. life
5. school
6. work
7.

(at least once
    every day.)

2. Always look for
   the good in others...

looking for  in others

(No matter what it takes !)

3. And never stop
   believing in yourself...

I do
believe in
me!

(Not even for a second!)

A B C

1 2 3

They've brought you
to this place
today

60

3
2
1
C
B
A

where the future
waits beneath your feet,

and where
the sky's
the limit!